ENERGY FOR THE FUTURE

ENERGY FROM WATER

by Christy Mihaly

T0361451

FOCUS
READERS.
NAVIGATOR

WWW.FOCUSREADERS.COM

Copyright © 2022 by Focus Readers®, Lake Elmo, MN 55042. All rights reserved. No part of this book may be reproduced or utilized in any form or by any means without written permission from the publisher.

Focus Readers is distributed by North Star Editions:
sales@northstareditions.com | 888-417-0195

Produced for Focus Readers by Red Line Editorial.

Content Consultant: Darrin Magee, Professor of Environmental Studies, Hobart and William Smith Colleges

Photographs ©: Shutterstock Images, cover, 1, 4–5, 7, 8–9, 11, 12–13, 15, 17, 18–19, 22, 25, 29; Simon Waldman/Alamy, 21; Orbital/Cover Images/AP Images, 26–27

Library of Congress Cataloging-in-Publication Data
Names: Mihaly, Christy, author.
Title: Energy from water / by Christy Mihaly.
Description: Lake Elmo, MN : Focus Readers, [2022] | Series: Energy for the future | Includes index. | Audience: Grades 4-6
Identifiers: LCCN 2021033811 (print) | LCCN 2021033812 (ebook) | ISBN 9781637390603 (hardcover) | ISBN 9781637391143 (paperback) | ISBN 9781637391686 (ebook) | ISBN 9781637392171 (pdf)
Subjects: LCSH: Water-power--Juvenile literature.
Classification: LCC TC147 .M54 2022 (print) | LCC TC147 (ebook) | DDC 621.31/2134-dc23
LC record available at https://lccn.loc.gov/2021033811
LC ebook record available at https://lccn.loc.gov/2021033812

Printed in the United States of America
Mankato, MN
012022

ABOUT THE AUTHOR

Christy Mihaly has written more than 25 books for young readers. She covers science, technology, public policy, and environmental issues. Christy delves into the wonders of water in her 2021 book, *Water: A Deep Dive of Discovery*. She lives and writes by a babbling brook in Vermont.

TABLE OF CONTENTS

CHAPTER 1

THE POWER OF WATER

Moving water can be very powerful. It is easy to see this power at Niagara Falls. The wide Niagara River runs from Lake Erie to Lake Ontario. It flows along the border between New York State and Ontario, Canada. At one point, the river crashes down a cliff more than 180 feet (55 m) high. This is Niagara Falls.

Niagara Falls is actually three waterfalls. The American Falls and Bridal Veil Falls are in the United States. The Horseshoe Falls is in Canada.

At the falls, the air fills with a thundering roar. Rainbows float in the mist. Approximately 748,000 gallons (2.8 million L) of water pour over the edge every second. It would take 25 years for the average American to use that much water.

Tourists visit the falls for their impressive beauty. But behind the scenes, something else is happening. People are harnessing the water's power.

Hydroelectric power plants are located above and below Niagara Falls. They use the river's flow to make electricity. They produce enough power to light up millions of homes.

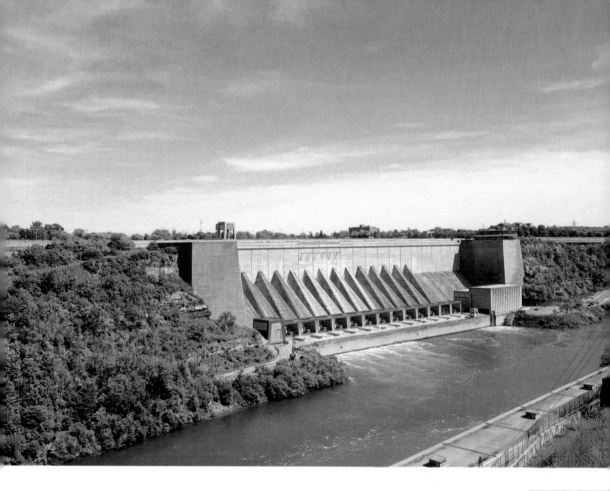

Five plants generate electricity from the Niagara River. Two are in the United States, and three are in Canada.

Water makes these plants run. But the water is not used up. It returns to the river. In this way, water is a **renewable energy** source. It is also clean. It is an important energy source for the future.

CHAPTER 2

WAVES AND WATER WHEELS

People have been putting water to work since ancient times. Two thousand years ago, the Romans built water mills to make flour. The mills had large wheels with paddles around the edges. Water flowing onto the wheels made them spin. The wheels turned giant stones, which ground grains into flour.

In what is now France, the ancient Romans built the Barbegal water mills. Raised channels called aqueducts brought water to 16 mills.

In the Middle Ages, Europeans powered mills with ocean tides. Tides are the regular rise and fall of ocean levels along shores. Tide-powered mills often used **reservoirs** or ponds that filled at high tides. As the tides fell, water flowed from the reservoirs to turn the water wheels.

In the late 1800s, people started using electric lights. They needed a regular

SU SONG'S WATER CLOCK

In the late 1000s, a Chinese inventor built a water clock. It was 40 feet (12 m) high. It used a water wheel lined with buckets. Water ran from a tank onto the wheel. When a bucket filled, it turned the wheel. The next bucket moved into place to be filled.

La Venera tide mill in Spain had 13 wheels that turned as water was released from the reservoir.

source of electricity. Inventors such as Nikola Tesla developed ways to produce electric power. Tesla designed one of the earliest hydroelectric plants. It opened in 1896 at Niagara Falls.

Today, more than one billion people use power from hydroelectric plants. And scientists are developing new ways to get electricity from water.

CHAPTER 3

ELECTRICITY FROM RIVERS

A hydroelectric plant often includes a dam. The dam blocks a river and creates a reservoir or lake. People release the water as needed to generate electricity.

The released water flows down. It pushes against the blades of a **turbine**. This machine connects to a **generator**.

The height of the water and the strength of the water's flow determine how much electricity is produced at a hydroelectric plant.

Turning the turbine spins the generator. This action produces an electrical current. The electricity is sent to homes and businesses.

Hydroelectricity has many benefits. First, it is renewable. After turning the turbines, the water returns to the river. It eventually flows to the ocean. Water

TYPES OF PLANTS

Most US hydroelectric plants use dams. These walls store water upstream of the plants. Other plants are built across rivers. The rivers flow through the plants. They turn turbines without creating reservoirs. At either kind of plant, electricity flows along power lines. It goes to where people need it.

evaporates, then falls again as rain. This water cycle keeps Earth's water flowing.

Also, hydroelectric plants do not burn **fossil fuels**. So, they do not add **greenhouse gases** to the air. These are gases that cause **climate change**.

HYDROELECTRICITY

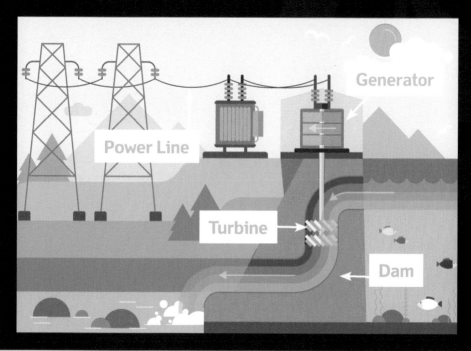

Dams and reservoirs can provide other benefits. They store water for people to use. People can swim and boat in some reservoirs. Furthermore, dams can protect people from floods. A dam can slow the flow of water downstream in big storms. It can stop the river from overflowing.

But dams also cause problems. The concrete used to build them produces huge amounts of greenhouse gases. Also, creating a reservoir means flooding large areas of land. Sometimes whole towns end up underwater. People and animals lose their homes. And the plants there die. They rot and release gases. One is methane, a powerful greenhouse gas.

Dams on the Columbia River flooded villages and destroyed fishing sites used by Indigenous peoples of the Pacific Northwest.

Finally, hydroelectricity can harm fish. The water in reservoirs is warmer than in rivers. This harms many fish. Some fish die in turbines. Also, fish such as salmon swim upriver to lay their eggs. The dams stop them. This can kill off the fish populations people depend on for food. Some dams have fish ladders to help fish swim up around the dams. But most ladders have not been very effective.

CHAPTER 4

THE WAVE OF THE FUTURE

The ocean is always in motion. Its tides and waves contain vast amounts of energy. People are finding ways to turn that energy into electricity.

Tidal power plants use the tide's flow to spin turbines. At some plants, underwater turbines and generators sit in long structures. These are built across narrow

As of 2021, South Korea had the largest tidal power project in the world. It uses the Yellow Sea's high tides to generate electricity.

bays or openings to the ocean. Another system places turbines on the ocean floor where tides are strong. Still other tidal power devices float on the surface.

Getting electricity from waves is more challenging. Waves form when wind blows along the ocean's surface. The wind is irregular. So, waves are irregular, too. Inventors have tried many designs to produce electricity from waves.

Some wave-power devices float like long snakes on the water. Some are attached to shore. Others sit on the ocean floor. All of these systems use waves to move pumps or turbines to create electricity.

The Pelamis P2 device has sections that can bend and move in the waves. Generators inside each section turn the movement into electricity.

Harnessing ocean power is not easy. Conditions at sea are rough. It is hard to move devices into place at sea. And the equipment must be very sturdy. This is because salt water causes metal to rust.

There are other challenges, too. Building these machines is expensive. Also, getting the electricity to shore

Turbines spin with the tide's movement.

means setting up expensive undersea cables. Ocean-power equipment is sometimes noisy, too. That can bother people near the shore and animals at sea. Animals could also be sucked into the turbines. For all these reasons, the ocean is not yet a major source of power.

But ocean power has great potential. The ocean's supply of tides and waves is endless. And tides are reliable. People can plan the next 15 years of tides without error. Scientists will keep working on the technology to meet the challenges.

OCEAN POWER FROM HEAT

The ocean's surface is warmer than deep water. New technology uses this temperature difference to make electricity. A device with a closed loop of tubing is placed in the ocean. The tube is filled with a liquid such as ammonia. Ammonia has a low boiling point. Warm surface water turns the ammonia into steam. The steam spins turbines and runs generators. Then the ammonia is cooled with water from the deep. It returns to liquid form and is reused.

THE ORKNEY ISLANDS

Orkney is a group of islands off the coast of Scotland. The ocean there is wild. People are putting its power to good use.

Orkney leads the world in ocean-power research. Designers test ideas there. They see if devices can survive the rough Orkney waters. If so, the devices will likely do well in gentler seas elsewhere.

The Orkney Islands produce all their electricity from renewable sources. These sources include wind, solar, and ocean power. Orkney makes more electricity than the people there need. Underwater cables send extra power to the mainland. But the cables cannot carry all the electricity these islands produce.

Rough ocean waters help the Orkney Islands produce 120 percent of the electricity they need.

So, the people of Orkney have found ways to use their extra electricity. By driving electric cars, they can use less gasoline. By switching to electric heat, they can use less heating oil. Orkney is leading the way toward a future free of fossil fuels.

CHAPTER 5

RESERVOIRS OF RENEWABLE POWER

Hydroelectric plants on rivers have produced electricity for more than 100 years. Ocean-power technology is newer. Both types of water power are important for Earth's future. But there are challenges ahead.

Building new dams is difficult. Dams are expensive. And many people oppose

In 2021, the O2 floating tidal turbine launched. It was cheaper to produce than other tidal turbines on the market.

damming rivers. Dams can flood farms and destroy towns. They can kill fish and damage river systems.

One answer is to get more power from old dams. Some dams were built to control flooding. They do not generate electricity. But hydroelectric generators can be added to them.

Ocean-power technology faces different problems. It is just getting started. Engineers are still figuring out the best designs and materials.

Developing new energy sources takes years. Research is expensive. For example, governments spent billions of dollars on wind and solar energy between

Norway gets more than 90 percent of its electricity from hydropower.

2005 and 2015. Now, many are turning their attention to water power.

The reason is clear. Water covers 71 percent of Earth. It is a valuable source of renewable energy. Using more renewable energy means using fewer fossil fuels. That is an important step in slowing climate change. Water power is key to Earth's energy future.

FOCUS ON
ENERGY FROM WATER

Write your answers on a separate piece of paper.

1. Write a paragraph summarizing the main ideas of Chapter 3.

2. What type of water power technology do you think is the most interesting? Why?

3. In which part of a hydroelectric plant is an electrical current produced?

   A. the turbine
   B. the generator
   C. the reservoir

4. What is a likely reason that people do not get much electricity from the ocean?

   A. Most people are afraid of the ocean.
   B. The ocean is too small to make much power.
   C. The technology is new and expensive.

Answer key on page 32.

GLOSSARY

climate change
A human-caused global crisis involving long-term changes in Earth's temperature and weather patterns.

evaporates
Changes from liquid to gas.

fossil fuels
Energy sources that come from the remains of plants and animals that died long ago.

generator
A machine that turns the energy of motion into electricity.

greenhouse gases
Gases that trap heat in Earth's atmosphere, causing climate change.

hydroelectric
Relating to the generation of electricity using water.

renewable energy
Energy produced from a source that will not run out.

reservoirs
Human-made lakes used for water supply storage.

turbine
A wheel that is turned by water, steam, or air and used to produce power.

TO LEARN MORE

BOOKS

Brearley, Laurie. *Water Power: Energy from Rivers, Waves, and Tides.* New York: Scholastic, 2019.

Clark, Stacy. *Planet Power: Explore the World's Renewable Energy.* Concord, MA: Barefoot Books, 2021.

Hirsch, Rebecca E. *Climate Change and Energy Technology.* Minneapolis: Lerner Publications, 2019.

NOTE TO EDUCATORS

Visit **www.focusreaders.com** to find lesson plans, activities, links, and other resources related to this title

INDEX

Answer Key: **1.** Answers will vary; **2.** Answers will vary; **3.** B; **4.** C